Text copyright © 1986 Beverley Parkin
This edition copyright © 1987 Lion Publishing

Published by
Lion Publishing plc
Icknield Way, Tring, Herts, England
ISBN 0 7459 1356 3
ISIS Large Print Books
55 St Thomas' Street, Oxford, England
ISBN 1 85089 210 5
Albatross Books Pty Ltd
PO Box 320, Sutherland, NSW 2232, Australia
ISBN 0 86760 901 X

First edition 1986
Reprinted 1986, 1987
This large print edition 1987
Reprinted 1992

Bible quotations from *The Holy Bible, New International Version:*
copyright © New York International Bible Society, 1978

Acknowledgments
Cover photograph by Picturebank
Text photographs by S. & O. Mathews with additional photographs
by Alan Beaumont, Wallflowers, Holly; John Feltwell, Fuchsias;
Sonia Halliday Photographs/F.H.C. Birch, Gladiolus,
Sonia Halliday, Violets; Lion Publishing/David Alexander,
endpapers, Gentian, Heart's-ease Pansies; Sutton Seeds, Torquay, Carnations

Printed and bound in Slovenia

Flowers with love

BEVERLEY PARKIN

LION · LARGE PRINT EDITIONS

Tulips

Tulips are at their best en-masse, great companies of them filling flower-beds, dressed in different coloured uniforms. There are fantastic displays of massed tulips at the Kirkennof Gardens in Holland.

Placed near a window indoors, however, and turned a fraction every day, tulip stems will twist and turn, seeking the source of light.

There are times in our lives when we desperately seek for a solution to a problem, twisting and turning, spending sleepless nights, exhausted by nervous strain. But if, like the tulips, we seek the light for a way through our problems we shall find real relief from our anxieties.

"Jesus said, 'I am the light of the world. Whoever follows me will never walk in darkness, but will have the light of life.'"
FROM JOHN'S GOSPEL, CHAPTER 8

Gladiolus

The regal queen of flowers, the gladiolus, presides over the herbaceous border surveying her lesser subjects.

Gladioli have the spiky shape ideal for an arrangement outline, providing a strong background for other flowers. I place the first gladiolus in position in a triangle arrangement and then insert the other stems so that they angle in towards the first bloom. This centre flower is the guide for all the other blooms and foliage.

We all have our pride, and we like to depend on our own resources. But Jesus asks for the central position in our lives. He is our guide and example and we shall not go far wrong if all our thoughts and actions are referred to him.

"Trust in the Lord with all your heart and lean not on your own understanding; in all your ways acknowledge him, and he will make your paths straight."
FROM PROVERBS, CHAPTER 3

Thrift

After all the storms of winter in Scotland it seems miraculous that the cliffs are so soon covered with a cloak of pink flowers. The little clumps of thrift or sea pinks cling tenaciously to nooks and crannies over the cliff face. The north winds threaten to tear out the little plants yet they thrive and blossom.

Jesus never promised us that life would be easy. But God has a special purpose for each of our lives and he will give us strength to withstand hardships as we trust him.

"Everyone who hears these words of mine and puts them into practice is like a wise man who built his house on the rock. The rain came down, the streams rose, and the winds blew and beat against that house; yet it did not fall, because it had its foundation on the rock."

FROM MATTHEW'S GOSPEL, CHAPTER 7

Gentian

Several years ago my husband and I visited Switzerland. I badly wanted to find gentians growing in the high pastures.

Thanks to my bad navigation we once found ourselves on a very narrow track, with the car wheel inches away from a sheer precipice.

This little incident made me realize how easy it is to lose our way in ordinary daily living. There are so many grey areas, situations in which it is difficult to know how to act. It's at times like this that I am especially glad of the 'map' God has provided. I can turn to the Bible and find guidance and help.

"All Scripture is God-breathed and is useful for teaching, rebuking, correcting and training in righteousness, so that the man of God may be thoroughly equipped for every good work."
FROM PAUL'S SECOND LETTER TO TIMOTHY, CHAPTER 3

Magnolia

Behind partially closed curtains in my hospital ward was an elderly woman named Annie – I have never seen anyone so crippled and twisted with arthritis. Her joints stood out grotesquely, all over her body, and the slightest movement gave her great pain. Yet I never heard her complain. She was caring towards the nurses throughout their ministrations.

Now, whenever I see a magnolia – old, gnarled and twisted – putting forth its fragrant, perfect waxen blossoms, I am reminded of Annie.

Jesus thought and prayed for others, even as the soldiers hammered nails into his hands and he hung on the cross in agony. Only the sustaining strength and love of God himself can enable us to cope with our pain and suffering without bitterness.

"O Lord, do not forsake me; be not far from me, O my God."
FROM PSALM 38

Honeysuckle

On warm evenings in late spring, the perfume of the honeysuckle scents the air. It looks a terrible mess in winter, but suddenly the mass of scrawny, dead-looking stems bursts into a haze of green, pink and cream.

People, like the honeysuckle, can seem dead, brittle and hard – perhaps because they are hurting inside. But God's love can warm and reach into the very depths of our being, touching and transforming our cramped spirits, until once again there is a surge of new life. Whenever we feel 'dead' inside and unable to tell others, we can talk to God about it and ask for his help. And we can look for the answer! It may be a long wintry wait, but it will come as surely as the flower in the wood – the honeysuckle.

"The Lord is close to the brokenhearted and saves those who are crushed in spirit."
FROM PSALM 34

Bluebells

Is there anything more beautiful than a bluebell wood? The swathes of blue and the elusive perfume cannot fail to touch the senses. The soft green beech leaves soar above, allowing the sun to highlight every delicate bell.

It is one of my favourite places to walk and pray. Many problems have been shared with God, and praises given, among the bluebells. Do those in our lane who walk their dogs in the wood go there to pray, too, I wonder? I know that some do so. But the bluebells keep their own counsel – and our secrets – in that marvellous place of tranquillity and peace.

"Do not be anxious about anything, but in everything, by prayer and petition, with thanksgiving, present your requests to God."

FROM PAUL'S LETTER TO THE
PHILIPPIANS, CHAPTER 4

Phlox

Two colourful prints hang on our dining-room wall; the artist obviously loved cottage gardens, and both pictures depict cobbled paths and thatched roofs. Nasturtiums, hollyhocks, delphiniums, roses and tree-mallow, rudbeckia, phlox and irises bloom in an everlasting summer along the paths.

It is enticing to live in a pretend world of perpetual summer, to shut our eyes to the real world about us. But life is not perfect and never will be until Jesus comes again. In the meantime he expects us to grasp reality and deal with it.

"As the soil makes the sprout come up and a garden causes seeds to grow, so the Sovereign Lord will make righteousness and praise spring up before all nations."
FROM ISAIAH CHAPTER 61

Violets

When my mother and father began courting, their first walk together took them in search of the violet, and, for the rest of their married life, father presented mother with a nosegay of violets on the anniversary of their first walk together.

Such a little, unobtrusive flower, the violet nestles under its leaves. Searching for the purple heads is like taking part in a treasure hunt.

It is remarkably easy in life to forget the little things that can mean so much – the warm embrace, the timely letter, the unexpected phone-call, or sympathetic ear. Violets increase through being picked, and the small gestures of love start ripples which may have a greater impact than we can ever imagine.

"Dear children, let us not love with words or tongue but with actions and in truth."

FROM THE FIRST LETTER OF JOHN,
CHAPTER 3

Meadow Grass

I believe God has a great sense of humour! Who but God would choose an ordinary woman with one useless arm to arrange flowers in front of hundreds of people and share with them the good news about him? God is constantly telling us, in every way possible, that our weakness is his strength and that he loves and uses imperfect, insignificant people to spread the word of his forgiveness and love.

In the natural world, meadow grass is of immense value to all the creatures that depend on it. It gives them sustenance and life. Here, too, God uses ordinary, insignificant elements of his creation to play a vital, life-giving role.

"My grace is sufficient for you, for my power is made perfect in weakness."

FROM PAUL'S SECOND LETTER TO THE CORINTHIANS, CHAPTER 12

Lilies

There is a beautiful bay in Turkey: the brilliant blue sea is surrounded by pine-clad hills. White lilies grow in the sand to the sea's edge and hundreds of small white snails make their home among the stems.

One night, after a violent storm, the sea swept in assorted debris and litter – plastic bags, bottles and dozens of shoes covered the beach. Some of the lilies continued to bloom pathetically above plastic-wrapped stems.

The unforgettable sight of those beautiful white lilies is a constant personal reminder to care for God's world, and to fill my mind with things that are wholesome and good.

"Whatever is true, whatever is noble, whatever is right, whatever is pure, whatever is lovely, whatever is admirable . . . think about such things."

FROM PAUL'S LETTER TO THE
PHILIPPIANS, CHAPTER 4

Wallflowers

When I was a little girl, I used to visit an aunt who possessed a magnificent oil painting of wallflowers in a bowl. When I stood on tiptoe, right in front of it, all I could see was a mass of colour. But, standing back, the design of the rich, velvety wallflowers sprang into focus.

This lovely painting made a deep impression on me and, when we established our first home, I was thrilled to find wallflower-printed furnishing fabric, now alas scuffed into oblivion by the children's sandals and wriggling bottoms!

I learned a lesson from the wallflower picture. If I step back and look at our chaotic and confusing world, through God's eyes, it is possible even now to see something of the beauty he originally intended and which he will one day restore.

"God saw all that he had made, and it was very good."
FROM GENESIS, CHAPTER 1

Fuchsias

There is one particular flower I find fascinating: the fuchsia.

There are ballerina frills and slinky skirts, long sinewy petals and short perky ones. It is amazing that one flower family can produce such incredibly different shapes and colours.

The Christian family is like the fuchsia family in its infinite variety. It is a wide family of different nations, different cultures – all united because we belong to Jesus. God does not force us into one mould. He delights in variety – every person different and special. Each bringing something unique to the whole family.

"Accept one another, then, just as Christ accepted you, in order to bring praise to God."
FROM PAUL'S LETTER TO THE ROMANS, CHAPTER 15

Carnations

Recently my nephew – tired from a long aeroplane flight – gave three silk carnations from his new brother and himself to the grandmother they had never seen before. What a loving introduction. As the children returned home the little silk flowers remained to remind their grandmother of the strands of love spanning the distance.

God our Father opens his arms to welcome new members into his family. He asks us, not for gifts or flowers, but to give ourselves, trusting him to receive us. Jesus has left us a remembrance and a promise of reunion with him. As we taste the wine and eat the bread at the communion service our hearts warm to the knowledge of the depth and breadth of God's love and concern for us all.

"And he took bread, gave thanks and broke it, and gave it to them, saying, 'This is my body given for you; do this in remembrance of me.'"
FROM LUKE'S GOSPEL, CHAPTER 22

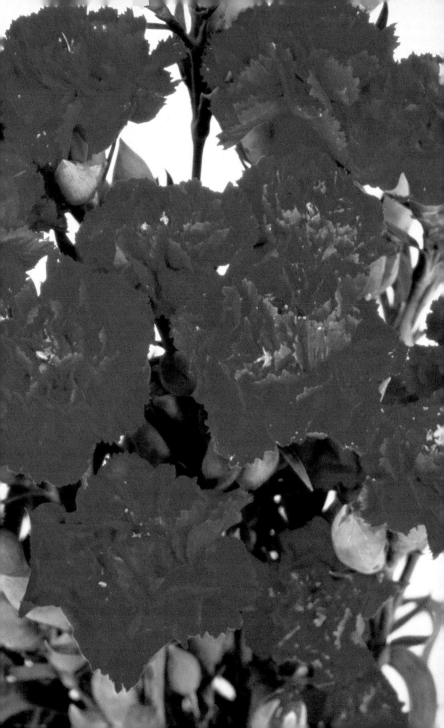

Heart's-ease Pansies

Tiny flowers with miniature faces, heart's-ease pansies grow close to the ground. Their purple, yellow and white blooms look up, waiting to be recognized and acknowledged. Left to themselves they flourish and grow into large families, ignoring their more flamboyant cultivated sisters.

My grandmother loved pansies; the heart's-ease was her favourite. She said they looked so cheerful, whatever the weather – a lesson for us, perhaps.

The heart's-ease, by its name, reminds us to become channels through which God can show love and compassion to those whose minds are ill-at-ease. In this way, we follow the example of Jesus.

"When Jesus saw the crowds, he had compassion on them, because they were harrassed and helpless, like sheep without a shepherd."
FROM MATTHEW'S GOSPEL, CHAPTER 9

Heather

You really have to get down on your knees to study the tiny flowers of the low-growing Erica family, yet each one contributes to the overall effect of a purple or white spray.

It reminds me of a visit we made to a group of young people, all badly disabled. These young men and women all loved Jesus. Although some were stunted in growth, their spiritual life was full-bodied and strong.

It is tempting to write off as useless all that is not perfect. But how wrong we are. Not all the heather bells are perfect but, integrated with others, they bring beauty into our lives. And these disabled friends of mine enriched my perception of God's blessing.

"God chose the lowly things of this world and the despised things . . . so that no one may boast before him."
FROM PAUL'S FIRST LETTER TO THE
CORINTHIANS, CHAPTER 1

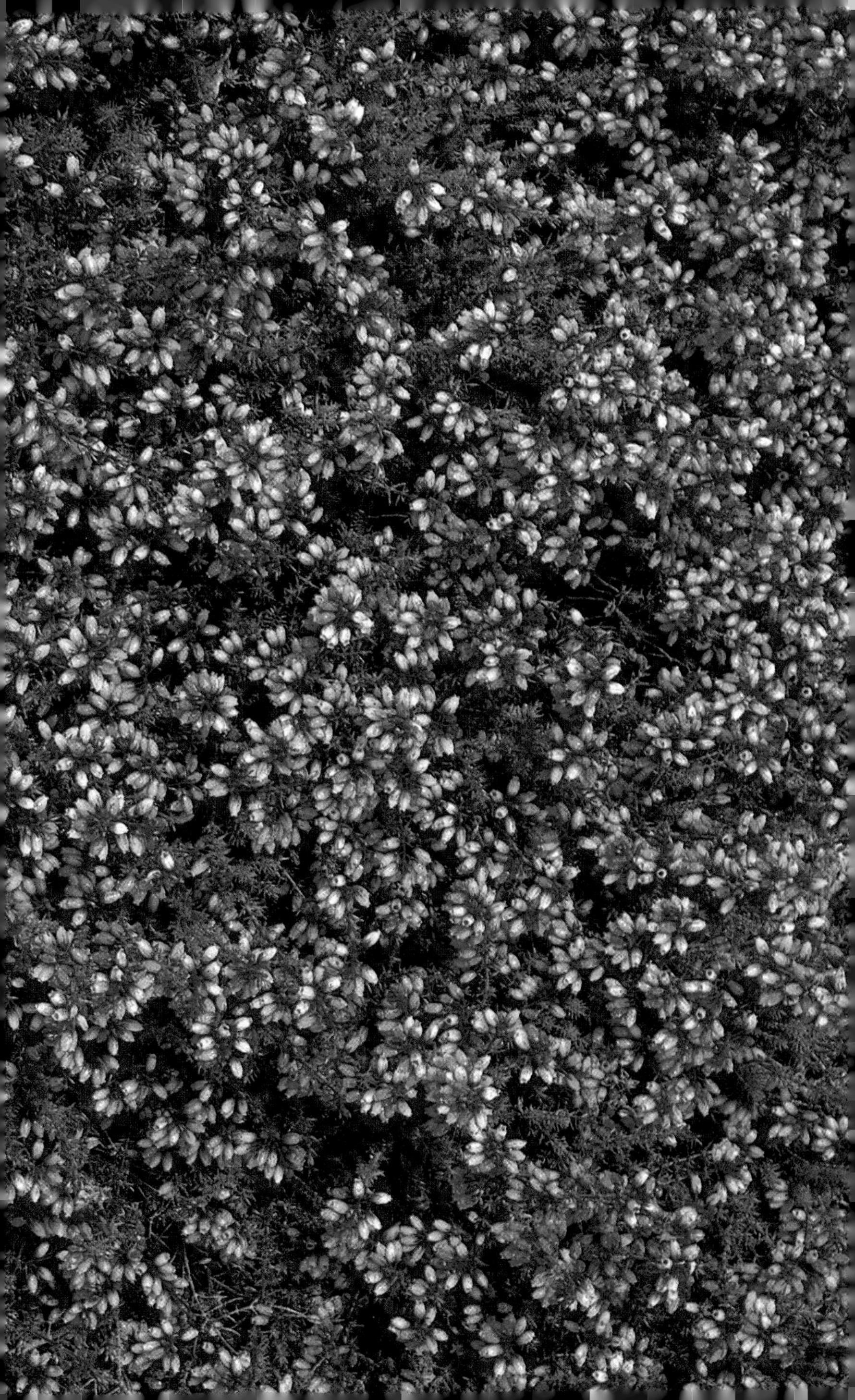

—Rosehips and Wild Clematis—

The sweet fresh scents and the low autumnal sunshine illuminate a new aspect of the natural world about us. Plant stems and leaves throw long shadows and flower-heads glisten with silvery dew. The leaves of maple and beech shiver and float gently to the ground, settling into a patterned carpet before they dry and crisp beneath our feet. Jewelled necklaces of berries tangle with the spiral-headed clematis, as it begins to burst into fluffy white seedheads.

When does our own 'autumn' begin? My first white hairs came in my twenties.

But the autumnal world of plant and human life has its own beauty. There is still a positive role for the older ones among us. We all need the wisdom and illumination which they can provide.

"Even when I am old and grey, do not forsake me, O God."
FROM PSALM 71

Dahlias

A wedding brings great changes into a family – in our own case, a son given but a charming daughter gained. As we stood in the dahlia-decorated church, I reflected over the years that had passed so quickly. A tiny baby, a rampaging toddler, long-haired teenager and now a fully responsible young man beginning a new way of life.

For me that special day will always be linked with dahlias. A fragile head of petals held on a sturdy stem encourages me to think that although marriage too has its difficult, fragile moments there can be real strength in a relationship and commitment to one another which depends on mutual unselfishness and a growing trust in God.

"They are no longer two, but one. Therefore what God has joined together, let man not separate."
FROM MARK'S GOSPEL, CHAPTER 10

Holly

Most of us associate holly with Christmas decorations. The dark green, shiny leaves and red berries start beckoning my attention from October or November onwards. I usually forget to wear gloves, and the barbed leaves prickle and hurt, however gingerly they are carried.

Many of us tend to be prickly too. All too often we hurt one another. Misunderstandings and thoughtlessness can really get under our skins, not to mention the barbed remarks from our unruly tongues.

Christmas is a good time to remember God's message of peace to all humankind. With his help our lives can bear the fruit of love, patience and self-control, as berries on the holly bough.

"Whoever loves God must also love his brother."

FROM THE FIRST LETTER OF JOHN, CHAPTER 4

Gerbera

I have a special reason for choosing the gerbera to close this book. The gerbera, surrounded by lilies of the valley, was the centrepiece of my bridal bouquet. So it is a way of saying thank you to my· husband for his love, support and patience during the writing of these pages.

As a family, we have loved and grown together through crises and joys and during all these years we have been surrounded by God's love and faithfulness. God loves us all, not just as individuals, but as families, too, and he brings everyone who loves him into his worldwide family.

So now to you who have shared in my memories of family and home, I offer these flowers – with love.

"Put on love, which binds all virtues together in perfect unity."
FROM PAUL'S LETTER TO THE
COLOSSIANS, CHAPTER 3